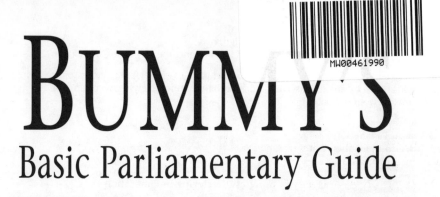

BUMMY'S
Basic Parliamentary Guide

An Illustrated Step-by-Step Procedure for Making Meetings Work

- Basics of Meeting Procedures • Recording Minutes: How, What, and Why
- Commonly Made Errors • Illustrated Dictionary of Parliamentary Signs

GERALD *"BUMMY"* BURSTEIN

DawnSignPress
San Diego, California

Bummy's Basic Parliamentary Guide
    Copyright © 1996, Gerald "Bummy" Burstein
    Sign illustrations copyright © 1996 DawnSignPress
    All rights reserved under International and Pan-American Copyright Conventions.

Producer: Joe Dannis
Sign Illustrator: Paul Setzer
Manufactured in the United States of America.
Published by DawnSignPress.

Library of Congress Cataloging-in-Publication Data

Burstein, Gerald, 1926-
    Bummy's basic parliamentary guide : an illustrated step-by-step
    procedure for making meetings work / Gerald "Bummy" Burstein.
        p.   cm.
    ISBN 0-915035-50-2 (alk. paper)
    1. Parliamentary practice. 2. Deaf—Means of communication.
I. Title.
JF515.B84 1996
060.4'2—dc21   96-48243
                                                              CIP

10   9   8   7   6   5   4   3   2   1

ATTENTION

Quantity discounts for organizations, schools,
distributors, and bookstores are available.
For information, please contact:
DawnSignPress
6130 Nancy Ridge Drive
San Diego, California 92121
619-625-0600 V/TTY 619-625-2336 FAX
ORDER TOLL FREE 1-800-549-5350

To my mentor

Charles H. "Charlie" Johnson, CPP

President 1994-1995
American Institute of Parliamentarians

TABLE OF CONTENTS

ACKNOWLEDGMENTS _vii_

FOREWORD _ix_

AUTHOR'S NOTE _xi_

SECTION ONE: Basics of Meeting Procedures _1_
    DEFINITIONS AND PURPOSES _3_
        The Words "Parliamentary" and "Procedure" _3_
        Parliamentary Procedure _4_
        The Principles of Parliamentary Procedure _5_
        The Purposes of Parliamentary Procedure _5_
        Four Democratic Principles _6_
    ORDER OF BUSINESS _6_
    EXAMPLES OF ORDER OF BUSINESS _7_
        Call to Order _7_
        Minutes _8_
        Treasurer's Report _9_
        Officers' Reports _9_
        Committee Reports _10_
        Unfinished Business _11_
        New Business _12_
        Announcements _13_
        Adjournment _13_

EIGHT STEPS IN MAKING A MAIN MOTION   *15*

AMENDMENTS   *18*

AMENDMENT TO A MOTION   *20*

NOMINATIONS   *24*

POINTS   *26*
    Point of Order   *26*
    Point of Inquiry   *27*
    Point of Information   *27*

SIMPLIFIED RANK OF BASIC MOTIONS   *28*

NON-RANKING MOTIONS   *28*

HELPFUL HINTS FOR COURTESY AND TACT   *29*

HELPFUL HINTS FOR THE PRESIDENT OR CHAIR   *30*

SECTION TWO: Recording Minutes   *31*
    Minutes   *33*
    Recording the Outcome of a Motion   *37*
    Sample Minutes   *38*

SECTION THREE: Commonly Made Errors   *43*
    Withdrawn Motion   *45*
    Close Debate   *47*
    Name of Seconder in the Minutes   *49*
    Adjournment   *51*

SECTION FOUR: Illustrated Dictionary of Parliamentary Signs   *53*

ABOUT THE AUTHOR   *93*

ACKNOWLEDGMENTS

The acknowledgments printed in the original booklet, *The Basics of Parliamentary Procedure,* also apply to this book. I again offer my appreciation to Gallaudet University Alumni Association (GUAA) board members Celia May Baldwin, a teacher at the California School for the Deaf, Fremont, and Donna Drake, supervising teacher of the high school department in the Florida School for the Deaf, for their valuable input and suggestions; to Rod Brawley, media specialist at the California School for the Deaf, Riverside, for his illustrations; to Dr. Charles H. Johnson, Certified Professional Parliamentarian of American Institute of Parliamentarians, for checking the parliamentary accuracy of this booklet; to Betty P. Ohlinger, a teacher at the California School for the Deaf, Riverside, for her editorial assistance; to Bertt Lependorf, a retired International Typographical Union printer, for his typographical advice and editorial assistance; to the California School for the Deaf, Riverside, for acceptance of this project as one of my professional goals; and to the GUAA for its inspiration, encouragement, and financial support of the original project and for distributing copies to schools and programs for deaf students throughout the United States.

For this book, Larry Fleischer, Susan Margolin, Sharon and Mel Carter, Jr., and Joyce R. Linden formed a committee to discuss the parliamentary signs. Mel Carter, Jr. was a valuable consultant for the sign illustrations. Much appreciation goes to the committee and especially to Mel for his patience and special contribution.

Additional appreciation goes to: Jane M. Klausman, CPP, who is a past secretary and past president of the American Institute of Parliamentarians, for reviewing the section on Recording Minutes, and for offering valuable suggestions; Charles H. Johnson, CPP, and Miriam Butcher, PRP, CPP, for checking this book from a parliamentary point of view for its accuracy; also, appreciation goes to Joyce R. Linden and Betty P. Ohlinger for checking this book from a non-parliamentary point of view for any needed clarification.

I am grateful to Joe Dannis of DawnSignPress for making this publication possible and for his suggestions and encouragement that led to the inclusion of more than was originally intended for the book. Above all, a very special thanks goes to the designer and copy editor, Tina Jo Breindel, for her patience, encouragement, and suggestions in the development of this book.

Gerald "Bummy" Burstein
Certified Professional Parliamentarian, AIP
Member, NAP

FOREWORD

GERALD "BUMMY" BURSTEIN has made a real contribution to parliamentary procedure in his publication, *Bummy's Basic Parliamentary Guide.* I have observed his development for quite a few years—having attended several American Institute of Parliamentarians (AIP) meetings with him, having been in attendance at his workshop, and having observed his oral examination for his Certified Professional Parliamentarian at the annual AIP session in Long Beach, California, in August, 1988.

Bummy has divided his book into four sections, namely (1) Basics of Meeting Procedures, (2) Recording Minutes, (3) Commonly Made Errors, and (4) Illustrated Dictionary of Parliamentary Signs.

SECTION ONE presents the usual standard procedure in a clear and simple format—including *Order of Business* at a meeting and *Eight Steps in Making Motions.* SECTION TWO includes why the minutes should be kept and the necessary content of minutes. SECTION THREE presents examples of common errors made during a meeting with ways to correct them. And finally, SECTION FOUR presents a dictionary of traditional and newly contrived illustrated signs to meet the needs of parliamentary procedure.

While the volume was designed especially as a guide for the meetings of deaf persons, giving signs to illustrate each step of parliamentary procedure for the conduct of a meeting, it has much to offer all students of parliamentary procedure. As designed, it is a must for the conduct of a meeting of deaf people.

Floyd M. Riddick,
Parliamentarian Emeritus,
United States Senate

AUTHOR'S NOTE

SINCE BOYHOOD, I have always been bothered by how meetings were handled. The more meetings I attended over the years, the more the various proceedings confused me. In addition to a parliamentary course at Gallaudet, I had studied Robert's Rules of Order on my own. In more recent years, I became so frustrated that I arranged for a tutor to teach me. My diligence paid off. I took and passed a written test with the National Association of Parliamentarians (NAP). Later I discovered another national parliamentary organization, the American Institute of Parliamentarians (AIP). I took a written test and a year later an oral test. I am now classified as a member of NAP and a Certified Professional Parliamentarian (CPP) of AIP. I am proud to say that I was the first deaf person to take these exams but not the first official deaf parliamentarian. That honor should go to Edwin Hazel. I have now served as a parliamentarian in various conventions: National Congress of Jewish Deaf (NCJD), California Association of the Deaf (CAD), National Association of the Deaf (NAD), and the Registry of Interpreters for the Deaf (RID). The RID convention was a unique experience for me because it was mainly a group of hearing people, with only a few deaf participants.

My original booklet, *The Basics of Parliamentary Procedure,* was written in June, 1986, for deaf students. About ten thousand copies have been printed and distributed through the kindness of the Gallaudet University Alumni Association. Although it was for deaf students, adults have been using it also. As far as I know, it is being used in three foreign countries.

As you can see, this book is divided into four sections: Basics of Meeting Procedures, Recording Minutes, Commonly Made Errors, and Illustrated Dictionary of Parliamentary Signs. The section on Basics of Meeting Procedures has been revised and rewritten to address all deaf people, adults and students, as well as interpreters.

At this writing, I have given more than 145 Parliamentary Procedure workshops for deaf students at schools and programs for the deaf and deaf adult communities. Many hearing people, mostly interpreters, also attended the workshops. At each workshop, questions were asked about the minutes and how to go about writing them. That prompted me to develop the second section on how to write the minutes. Sample models of minutes with a list of what should be in the minutes are shown in that section. One can select paragraphs that are applicable to specific situations as needed.

The third section is focused on common errors that were discussed at almost every workshop. The most common errors are related to withdrawn motions, closing debate, name of seconder in the minutes, and adjournment.

The idea for the fourth section, Illustrated Dictionary of Parliamentary Signs, originated with Sam Milesky, a Registered Parliamentarian with NAP and a retired State Supervisor of Programs for the Hearing Impaired in Wisconsin. His background also includes teaching at the Michigan School for the Deaf and serving as an interpreter.

A key example of how the dictionary of parliamentary signs can help you involves the word CHAIR. In the old days in England, when they had a meeting, there were benches in the meeting room where members sat. On the stage was a chair where the presiding officer sat.

The presiding officer was called the CHAIRMAN, which is now referred to as the CHAIR. In our sign language, we sign the word "chair" as a piece of furniture. We also use that sign for the presiding officer. Almost everywhere I go, I see that sign. The correct sign should be the one on page 64, fingers clawed on the shoulder to indicate the presiding officer as the Chair or the one in charge. Because the sign for chair (furniture) is so commonly used for the Chair (presiding officer), you will find it included in the dictionary of signs.

The sign "change" would be more accurate for AMEND or AMENDMENT on page 18 and page 57. We have retained the sign illustrated on those pages due to its common usage in meetings I have observed.

In the Illustrated Dictionary of Parliamentary Signs, one may notice that a few of the parliamentary terms have more than one sign. The illustrations are not intended to be in ranking order; therefore, one should feel free to select the sign that is most commonly used by the local population.

Keeping group meetings efficient is an age-old problem even under the best conditions. It is my fervent wish that this book will substantially help deaf and hearing people to communicate more clearly and achieve their goals more quickly than ever before when conducting business meetings together.

BUMMY'S
Basic Parliamentary Guide

SECTION 1

BASICS OF
MEETING PROCEDURES

DEFINITIONS AND PURPOSES

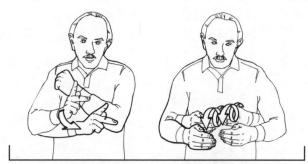

Parliamentary Procedure

What do the words PARLIAMENTARY and PROCEDURE mean?

PARLIAMENTARY - *According to the rules and customs that a group agrees to follow.*

PROCEDURE - *Way of doing things.*

What is PARLIAMENTARY PROCEDURE?

The members agree to a list of rules and customs. Each member has the right to speak and to be heard. Then the members vote to make a decision.

List

Vote

What are the PRINCIPLES of Parliamentary Procedure?

Principle

1. Courtesy to all.
2. Justice for all.
3. Rule of the majority.
4. Rights of the minority.
5. Favoritism to none.
6. One thing at a time.

What are the PURPOSES of Parliamentary Procedure?

1. To speed up business.
2. To keep order.
3. To ensure justice and equality for all.
4. To accomplish the purpose of the group.

Purpose

FOUR DEMOCRATIC PRINCIPLES

1. Recognize majority rule.
2. Protect the rights of the minority.
3. Protect the rights and privileges of the individual.
4. Protect the rights of absentees.

ORDER OF BUSINESS

The following is the order of business used in most meetings:

1. Call to Order
2. Minutes
3. Treasurer's Report
4. Officers' Reports
5. Committee Reports
6. Unfinished Business
7. New Business
8. Announcements
9. Adjournment

EXAMPLES OF ORDER OF BUSINESS

1. CALL TO ORDER

President: The meeting will please come to order.

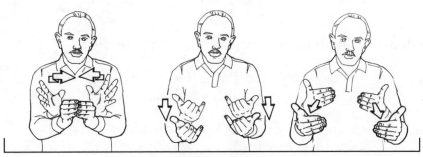

Call to order

2. MINUTES

President: The secretary will present the minutes of the previous meeting.
(Secretary distributes the minutes.)

President: Are there any corrections to the minutes?
(Seeing none.) The minutes are approved.

OR

President: Are there any corrections to the minutes?

Member A: There is an error. We at the last meeting voted to give $100 to the Naismith Club Banquet fund...not $50.

President: *(Pause for a few seconds.)* The correction is accepted.
Are there any further corrections?

(Seeing none.) The minutes are accepted as corrected.
(Note: no motion, no second)

3. TREASURER'S REPORT

President: We will now have a Treasurer's report.

President: Are there any questions? If none, the treasurer's report will be filed, subject to audit.

OR

President: *(After questions have been answered)* Are there any more questions? If none, the treasurer's report will be filed, subject to audit.

(Note: The assembly never votes to accept the treasurer's report. When the report of an auditing committee is adopted, the treasurer's report is automatically accepted.)

4. OFFICERS' REPORTS

President: I met with the Superintendent of the school about the rumors of closing the school. He assured me that the school will not close. The legislature is in full support of the school.

5. COMMITTEE REPORTS

The purposes of committees are:
   a.) to study a subject
   b.) to prepare recommendations
   c.) to carry out assignments
Committees may be appointed by the president or selected by the vote of members.

Chairman of the Dance Committee:

The Dance Committee has checked all the details and recommends a dance on Saturday night, June 1st, at the convention center. As Chair of the Dance Committee, I move that this recommendation be adopted.

(Note: No second is needed when the recommendation is made by a committee.)

Committees are appointed to act for the organization. During the meeting, it was agreed that the dance committee be authorized to plan a dance for June 1st because time did not permit the committee to report back at the next meeting for approval.

6. UNFINISHED BUSINESS *(Not old business)*

     a. Postponed motions
     b. Incomplete items from previous meeting

A motion was passed at the previous meeting to postpone until the next meeting the motion to sell T-shirts.

President: We have one item of unfinished business—the postponed motion from the previous meeting that we sell T-shirts.

Unfinished (Past) Business

President: Is there any discussion? *(Discussion, if any)*

President: Those in favor of the motion that we sell T-shirts, please raise your hand.

President: Those opposed to the motion, please raise your hand.

President: The motion to sell T-shirts is defeated. We will not sell T-shirts.

If there is no unfinished business:

President: Since we have no unfinished business, we shall now proceed to new business.

7. NEW BUSINESS

President: Is there any new business?

Members say: I move that . . . *or* I move to. . .

Do not say: I make a motion . . . *nor* I move you . . .

Member A: I move that we purchase a new red van.
(Second, debate and vote on)

8. ANNOUNCEMENTS

President: Are there any announcements?

Member A: There will be a first-run movie with captions next Wednesday at 7:00 p.m. in DSP theatre.

9. ADJOURNMENT

President: Since there is no further business, the meeting is adjourned.

OR

Member A: I move to adjourn.

Member B: Second.

President: It is moved and seconded that we adjourn.

President: Those in favor of the motion to adjourn, please raise your hand.

President: Those opposed to the motion, please raise your hand.

President: The motion to adjourn is carried (passed).

President: We are now adjourned.

EIGHT STEPS IN MAKING A MAIN MOTION

1. Raise your hand.
2. Wait until the President recognizes you.
3. Make the motion.

Member A: I move that we purchase a red van.

Say: I move that. . . *or* I move to . . .

Do not say: I make a motion . . . *nor* I move you . . .

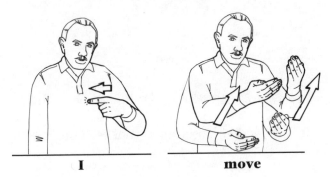

I	**move**

4. Another member seconds the motion.

Member B: I second the motion.

       OR

Member B: Second.

Second

5. The President *(the person conducting the meeting)* states *(repeats)* the motion.

President: It is moved and seconded that we purchase a red van.

6. The President asks for discussion.

    President: Is there any discussion?

7. The President puts the motion to vote.

    President: If you are in favor of the motion that we purchase a red van, please raise your hand.

    President: If you are against the motion, please raise your hand.

8. The President states the results of the vote and directs action.

    President: The motion is carried (passed). We will purchase a red van. Who would like to be on the committee to buy the new van?

(Or the president appoints a committee with no objection.)

AMENDMENTS

An amendment is a motion to change a pending motion.

Amend

MAIN MOTION: To buy a red van.

Ways to amend the motion:

1. By adding

Member A: I move to amend the motion by adding 'for not more than $23,000.'

2. By inserting

Member B: I move to amend the motion by inserting 'new' before 'red van.'

3. By striking out

Member C: I move to amend the motion by striking out 'red.'

4. By striking out and inserting

Member D: I move to amend the motion by striking out 'buy' and inserting 'lease.'

AMENDMENT TO A MOTION

Member A: I move that the Naismith Club sponsor a western dance on June 1st.

Member B: Second.

President: It is moved and seconded that the Naismith Club sponsor a western dance on June 1st. Is there any discussion?

(Discussion, if any)

Member C: I move to amend the motion by striking out "western" and inserting "costume."

Member D: Second.

President: It is moved and seconded to amend the motion by striking out "western" and inserting "costume." Is there any discussion?

(Discussion if any. Discussion is limited to amendment only, not on the main motion.)

Member E: I move to amend the amendment by striking out "costume" and inserting "formal."

Member F: Second.

President: It is moved and seconded to amend the amendment by striking out "costume" and inserting "formal." Is there any discussion?

(Discussion if any. Discussion is limited to amendment only.)

President: Since there is no more discussion, we will now vote on the amendment as amended.

Those in favor of striking out "costume" and inserting "formal," please raise your hand.

Those opposed, please raise your hand.

The amendment is carried.

President: Now the amendment as amended is striking out "western" and inserting "formal." Any discussion?

(Discussion, if any.)

President: Any further discussion?

Those in favor of striking out "western" and inserting "formal," please raise your hand.

Those opposed, please raise your hand.

The amendment as amended is carried.

President: Any discussion on the main motion as amended that the Naismith Club sponsor a formal dance on June 1st?

Member G: l move to close the debate.

Member H: I second it.

President: It is moved and seconded to close the debate.

This motion requires a two-thirds vote to close the debate.

Those in favor of closing the debate, please raise your hand.

Opposed, please raise your hand.

The motion to close debate is carried, with 35 in favor and 15 opposed.

President: We now vote on the main motion as amended, "That the Naismith Club sponsor a formal dance on June 1st."

Those in favor, please raise your hand.

Those opposed, please raise your hand.

The motion that Naismith sponsor a formal dance on June 1st is adopted.

President: The Dance Committee will be responsible for planning the formal dance.

NOMINATIONS

Nominations is the procedure used to nominate and elect officers.

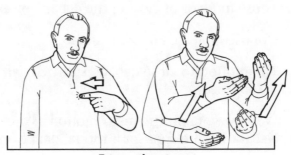

I nominate

President: We are now open for nominations for the office of president.

Member A: I nominate John Jones for president.
(No second is required.)

President: John Jones has been nominated for president. Are there any more nominations for president?

Member B: I nominate Mary Rice for president.
(No second is required.)

President: Mary Rice has been nominated for president. Are there any more nominations for president?

(Pause to wait for other nominations.)

President: If not, nominations for president are closed.

(Voting should be by ballot.)

John Jones received 23 votes. Mary Rice received 47 votes.

President: Mary has been elected president.
Congratulations, Mary.

President: We are now open for nominations for vice-president.

POINTS

Points are used to get the chair's attention when a member sees something is not right during the meeting or when a member needs information.

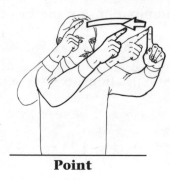

Point

Member A: *(interrupting)* Point of Order.

President: *(to Member A)* Please state (tell) your point.

Member A: The speaker is off the subject. The discussion is the kind of dance, not about the place.

President: Your point is well taken. Thank you.

OR

President: Your point is not well taken because both are equally important to each other.

Member B: *(interrupting)* Point of Inquiry.

President: *(to Member B)* Please state (tell) your point.

Member B: Will the convention center be available for the dance on June 1st?

President: The President will have to check on this.

Member C: *(interrupting)* Point of Information.

President: *(to Member C)* Please state (tell) your point.

Member C: The convention center is not available for the spring dance on June 1st.

Simplified Rank of Basic Motions

	REQUIRES SECOND	CAN BE DEBATED	CAN BE AMENDED	REQUIRES VOTE	CAN INTERRUPT
9. Adjourn	yes	no	no	majority	no
8. Recess	yes	no	yes	majority	no
7. Table	yes	no	no	majority	no
6. Close Debate	yes	no	no	2/3 vote	no
5. Limit Debate	yes	no	yes	2/3 vote	no
4. Postpone Definitely	yes	yes	yes	majority	no
3. Refer to Committee	yes	yes	yes	majority	no
2. Amend	yes	yes	yes	majority	no
1. Main Motion	yes	yes	yes	majority	no

Non-Ranking Motions

	REQUIRES SECOND	CAN BE DEBATED	CAN BE AMENDED	CHAIR'S DECISION	CAN INTERRUPT
Point of Order	no	no	no	yes	yes
Point of Information	no	no	no	yes	yes
Point of Inquiry	no	no	no	yes	yes

HELPFUL HINTS FOR COURTESY AND TACT

Courtesy

For the President:

> *Say:* The President. . .
> *Do not say:* I . . .

President: The President rules the motion out of order.

Do not say: I rule you out of order.

For the Members:

> Always wait until recognized by the President before speaking to the group.

HELPFUL HINTS FOR THE PRESIDENT OR CHAIR

President

Chair

1. Be brief.

2. Be a leader.

3. Be modest.

4. Speak with authority.

5. Ignore unimportant differences.

6. Keep an orderly meeting.

7. To control others, control yourself first.

8. Keep the assembly informed.

9. Communicate clearly.

RECORDING MINUTES
How, What, and Why

MINUTES

Why are minutes necessary?
1. Official permanent record and history of organization
2. Refresh memory of members on meeting action
3. Let absent members know meeting decisions
4. For reference

What should be in the minutes?
1. The kind of meeting:
   a. regular
   b. annual
   c. special
   d. adjourned

2. Name of the organization

3. Date – Time – Place

4. President and Secretary present or name of any substitute

5. Minutes of previous meeting approved as distributed/read or as corrected

6. A separate paragraph for each subject matter

7. Name of person who made a motion
   - No need to name those who seconded the motion

8. Result of each motion
   - Adopted or passed or carried
   - Lost or defeated
   - Disposal of by some other motion—such as postpone, refer, etc.

9. The number of votes on each side for any count or ballot

10. Last paragraph—time of adjournment

11. Minutes signed by Secretary and may be signed by President, with title

12. No need to use "Respectfully submitted." Respect is assumed.

13. A withdrawn motion is not recorded in the minutes. However, if the motion is postponed and at the next meeting it is withdrawn, it is recorded in the minutes in order to have a record of the disposition of the postponed motion.

14. Record what was done at the meeting, not what was said by the members.

15. The Secretary's opinion should never be reflected in the writing of the minutes.

16. All points of order and appeals are included, whether sustained or denied, together with the reasons given by the chair for the ruling.

17. When minutes are in the official minutes book, they are never erased or re-typed. If corrections are made, the Secretary circles or draws a line through part of the official minutes and makes corrections in the margin together with appropriate date and initials.

You may omit the name of the maker of amendments.

> The motion by Alissa that the club buy an electric typewriter
> was adopted as amended.
>
> *(It is not necessary to mention that Ronnie amended the motion to insert "electric.")*

You may omit the name of the maker who moves to table and/or to take
from the table.

> Sharon moved to buy a clubhouse. Mel moved to amend the
> motion by adding "with a swimming pool." The motion and the
> amendment were laid on the table.

Many organizations name the maker of the main motion only. They do
not name the maker of additional motions such as to amend, refer, close
debate, etc.

> The motion for a fifteen-minute recess was adopted.
>
> *(It did not name the maker of that motion.)*

RECORDING THE OUTCOME OF A MOTION

A	B
Motion adopted	Motion lost
Motion passed	Motion defeated
Motion carried	

Notice to Secretary: When you write the minutes, select one phrase from A and one phrase from B, and use the same phrases consistently throughout the minutes.

> *That is, if you select "Motion carried" and "Motion lost,"*
> *use these two throughout the minutes.*

> *Do not use:*
> *"Motion failed."*
> *"Motion not passed."*
> *"Motion not adopted."*
> *"Motion not carried."*

SAMPLE MINUTES

Associated Student Body Government (ASBG)

The regular meeting of ASBG was held in Room 413 at CSDR on Monday, January 8, 1996, at 1:30 p.m. President Mary Jones presided with Secretary Ann Lewis present.

A quorum of thirty–seven members was present with Mr. Thatcher as the sponsor.

The minutes of the previous meeting were approved as read.

The treasurer reported a balance of $435.37 as of December 31, 1995.

John Smith moved that the Riverside Chapter plan a trip to Knotts' Berry Farm on June 15th. Mary Collins moved to amend the motion by striking out "Knotts' Berry Farm" and inserting "Disneyland."

The amendment carried. The motion as amended carried.

Susan Perez, Chair of the Food Committee, moved that we request that the lunch menu include ice cream once a week. Motion carried. Susan Perez will meet with the dietitian.

The meeting was adjourned at 3:00 p.m.

Ann Lewis
Secretary

Naismith Club

The regular meeting of the Naismith Club was held at the DSP Center on June 13, 1996. President Tim Weiner called the meeting to order at 7:00 p.m. with the secretary, Gena Davis, being present.

A quorum of 47 members was present.

Minutes of the previous meeting were approved as distributed.

The treasurer reported a balance on hand of $3,859 on May 1st, receipts of $230 and expenditures of $525, which leaves a balance on hand of $3,564 as of May 31,1996.

Bob Crane, Chair of the Bylaws Committee, moved the following amendment to Article lll, Section 2, that dues for members be increased from $20 a year to $30 a year. The amendment passed with a two-thirds vote: 30 in favor, 12 against.

Joel Goldberg, Chair of the School Investigation Committee, presented a report on the status of emergency equipment. The report was filed.

Carol Lee, Chair of the Dinner-Dance Committee, moved that the dance be held on July 10th at the Hyatt Hotel at a cost of $100 per person and that it be a black-tie affair. The motion passed.

Marvin Lee, Chair of the Athletic Committee, moved that we sponsor the national basketball tournament in 1997. An amendment was made to have it in 1998. Amendment passed. The main motion as amended lost.

Carol Linden, Chair of the Sign Communications Committee, moved to spend $500 to sponsor a Deaf Culture Workshop. The motion was referred to the Budget Committee.

Under unfinished business, the motion postponed from the previous meeting, "that we sell T-shirts with the club's emblem," was presented. The motion lost.

John Escalera moved that our next meeting be held in Riverside, California. Mary Cardillo raised a point of order that the Bylaws give the power of meeting site selection to the Board. The President ruled that the decision must be made by the Board.

Diane Wagner moved that we recommend to the Board that the next convention be at Riverside. Betty Scarna moved to amend by striking out "Riverside" and inserting "San Francisco." Amendment passed. The main motion as amended passed.

Sidney Graubart moved that we buy a computer for office use. Charlie Carr moved to amend by inserting "Mac" before computer. Frances Fertik moved that the motion and amendment be referred to a committee of three appointed by the President to investigate the possibilities and report with a recommendation at the next meeting. Passed. The President appointed Joe Koen, Minnie Gold, and Hy Smith.

Gladys Acosta moved that we buy a red airplane. John Chen moved to postpone the motion to the next meeting. Passed.

There being no further business, by general consent the President adjourned the meeting at 11:00 p.m.

Gena Davis
Secretary

SECTION 3

COMMONLY MADE ERRORS

WITHDRAWN MOTION
(After discussion of a motion)

ERROR:

Member A: I withdraw my motion.

President to the Seconder:
> You agree to withdraw your second?

CORRECT:

Member A: I request that my motion be withdrawn.

President: There is a request by the maker of the motion that the motion be withdrawn. Is there any objection?

(PAUSE)

President: Since there is no objection, the motion is withdrawn.

OR

President: There is an objection to the motion being withdrawn. We shall vote now to decide if the motion will be withdrawn or not. It requires a majority vote. Those in favor of the motion being withdrawn, please raise your hand.

Those against, please raise your hand.

The majority is in favor. The motion is withdrawn.

CLOSE DEBATE

ERROR:

Member B:	I move to close the debate.
President:	Second?
Member C:	Second.
President:	It is moved and seconded to close debate.
	Those in favor of closing debate, please raise your hand.
	Those against, please raise your hand.
Member D:	I object to closing debate (or) I vote against closing debate.
President:	Since there is objection to closing debate, we will

(Some organizations continue debate if three people vote against closing debate. In other organizations, if one member votes against closing debate, the debate continues. Both are in error.)

CORRECT:

Member E: I move to close debate.

President: Any second? *(Seeing a second)*
It is moved and seconded to close debate.

To close debate requires a two-thirds vote. Those in favor of closing debate, please raise your hand.

Those against closing debate, please raise your hand.

Fifteen are in favor of closing debate and seven are against.

The motion to close debate is adopted. The vote is now on the main motion to. . .

NAME OF SECONDER IN THE MINUTES

ERROR:

Member F: I move that we spend a weekend in the country.

President: Second?

Member G: I second it.

President: It is moved and seconded that we spend a weekend in the country.

President to Secretary:
Member G seconds it.

To record the name of a seconder is not necessary. There are three reasons to second:

1. *The member is in favor of the motion.*

2. *The member is not sure of the motion. The member seconds it so that there will be debate to help decide how to vote.*

3. *The member does not like the motion, and seconds it in order to argue against it.*

Again, it is not necessary to name the person who seconds a motion in the minutes.

CORRECT:

Member F: I move to spend a weekend in the country.

President: Second?

(Seeing a second) It is moved and seconded that we spend a weekend in the country.

ADJOURNMENT

After new business and announcements, if any.

ERROR:

> **President:**   Since there are no further announcements, will someone please move to adjourn?
>
> *(It is not necessary to ask for adjournment.)*

CORRECT:

> **President:**   Are there any further announcements?
> *(Seeing none.)* The meeting is adjourned.

SECTION 4

ILLUSTRATED DICTIONARY OF PARLIAMENTARY SIGNS

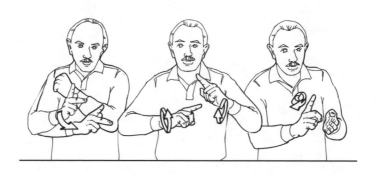

Illustrated Dictionary of Parliamentary Signs

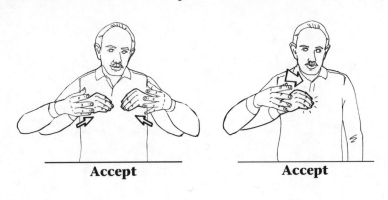

Accept
Accept

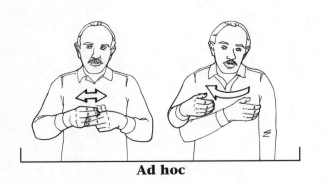

Ad hoc

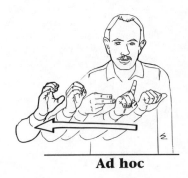

Ad hoc

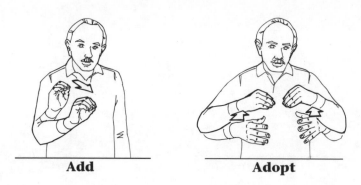

Add

Adopt

Adjourn

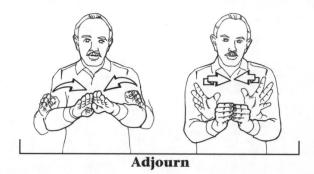

Adjourn

Agenda

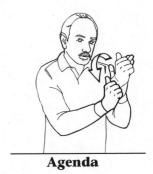

Agenda

**Amend (or)
Amendment**

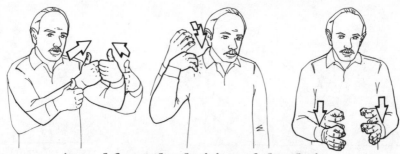

Appeal from the decision of the chair
(challenge the chair's decision)

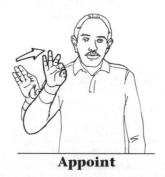

Appoint   **Appoint**   **Approve**

Article

Assembly

Audit

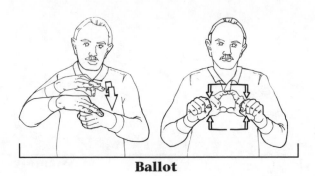

Ballot

Be it resolved

Board

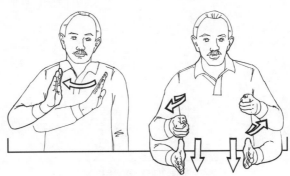

Board of Directors

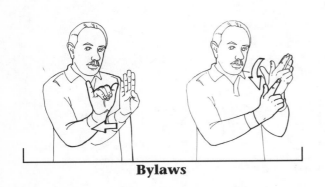

Bylaws

Bylaws

Call to order

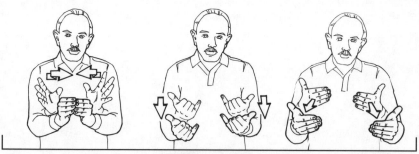

Call to order

Carried

Caucus

Chair

Chair

Close debate
(previous question)

Committee

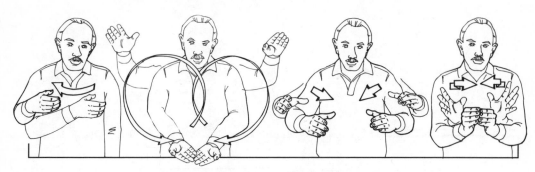

Committee of the whole

Consider

Constitution

65

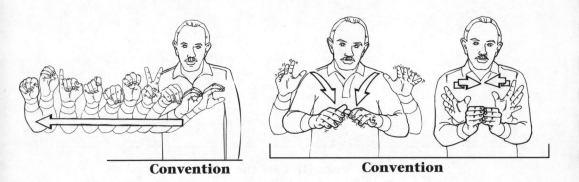

Convention

Convention

Corrections

Courtesy

Credentials

Debate

Defeated

Defeated

Delegates

Delegates

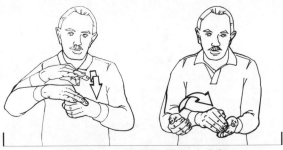

Division of the Assembly
(vote again)

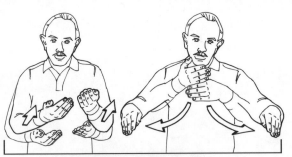

Division of a Question
(divide the motion)

Dues

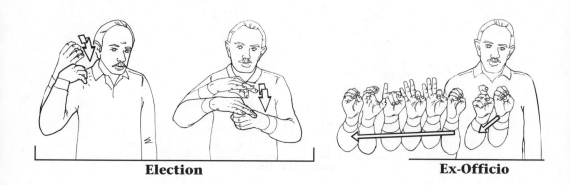

Election

Ex-Officio

Ex-Officio

Executive Board

Executive Board

Favor

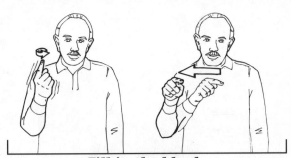

Fill in the blank

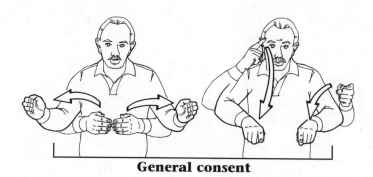

General consent

General consent

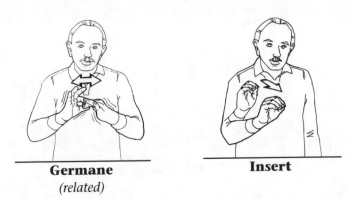

Germane
(related)

Insert

Main Motion

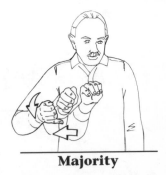

Majority

Meeting

Minority

Minutes

Minutes

Minutes

Motion

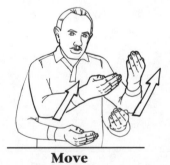

Move

New business

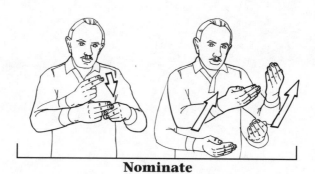

Nominate

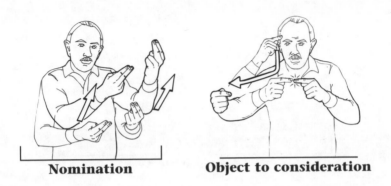

Nomination

Object to consideration

Officers

Oppose, Against

Oppose, Against

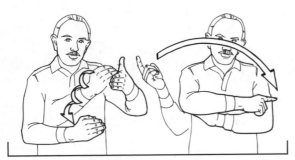

Orders of the day

Parliamentarian

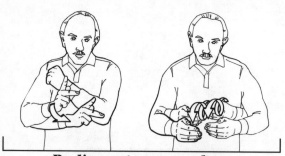

Parliamentary procedure

Passed

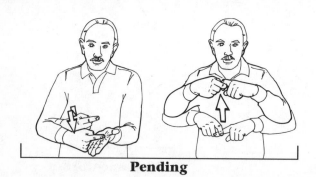

Pending

Pending

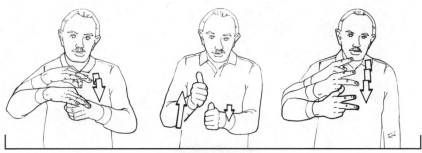

Plurality
(largest number of votes)

Point

Postpone

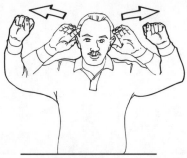

President

Principle

Procedure

Purpose

Rank

Ratify/Confirm

Recess

Recess

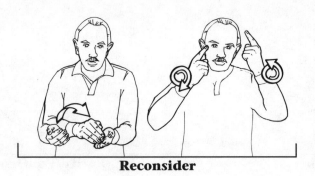

Reconsider

Refer

Refer

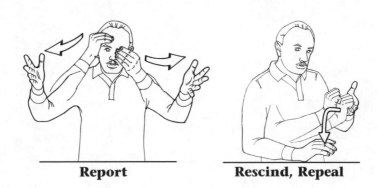

Report

Rescind, Repeal

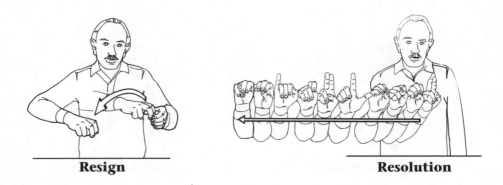

Resign

Resolution

Revision

Roll Call

Second

Secretary

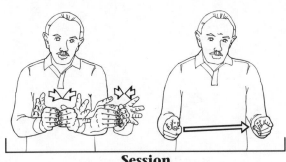

Session

Special committee

Standing committee

Standing order

Standing rules

Strike out

Strike out . . . and insert . . .

Substitute

Suspend

Table

Take from the table

Treasurer

Two-thirds (2/3)

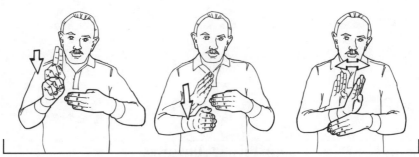

Unfinished business

Unfinished business

Unfinished business

Vice-president   **Vote**   **Whereas**

Withdraw   **Withdraw**

ABOUT THE AUTHOR

GERALD "BUMMY" BURSTEIN was born deaf and raised in Brooklyn, New York. In 1950, he obtained his Bachelor of Arts degree from Gallaudet University. In 1965, after teaching at the Minnesota School for the Deaf in Faribault for 15 years, he was admitted to the National Leadership Training Program at California State University, Northridge (CSUN), where he obtained his Master's degree in Administration and Supervision, and then joined the staff at the California School for the Deaf, Riverside. In 1994, he became a graduate of the first Leadership and Technology Management program at CSUN.

In his current position as Supervisor of Media Technology Services at CSDR, Bummy is now in his 47th year in the field of education of the deaf. He serves as West Coast Regional Manager and Depository Manager of the NAD Captioned Films/Videos Program at CSDR. He is also an adjunct teacher of Deaf Culture at Riverside Community College.

Bummy has served as president of the National Congress of Jewish Deaf, the California Association of the Deaf, and the Gallaudet University Alumni Association. He is in his 8th year as the only Chair of the Deaf and Disabled Telecommunication Administrative Committee of the California Public Utilities Commission since its inception. He is a member of the California Assistive Technology System Steering Council for the California Department of Rehabilitation, and also serves on the Consumer Advisory Board of the National Captioning Institute.

Many honors and awards have been bestowed upon Bummy in recognition of his various endeavors. On October 24, 1986, he received an Honorary Doctor of Laws Degree from Gallaudet University at the Convocation which officially marked Gallaudet's change from college status. He has also been inducted into the State of California Governor's Hall of Fame for People with Disabilities and into the National Congress of Jewish Deaf Hall of Fame. Bummy has received the International Platform Association Robert W. Leiman Silver Bowl for Popularizing Parliamentary Procedure and Gallaudet's Alice Cogswell Award for valuable service to the deaf community.

OTHER DAWNSIGNPRESS PRODUCTS

Personal Meaning In The Triumphs of a Deaf Celebrity

In this six-part video interview, Bernard Bragg brings viewers to laughter, tears, and offers them new meaning for their own lives. Born Deaf, Bragg learned mime from Marcel Marceau and went on to fame as an actor, playwright and director. He reveals feelings and experiences with enchanting wit and wisdom. A wonderful gift for Deaf and hearing alike.

An Interview with Bernard Bragg, The Man Behind the Mask
by Bernard Bragg and Tina Jo Breindel
Six-part video series ◆ voice-over

...More Hilarious Than Ever!

DEAF CULTURE, *Our Way* is now back by popular demand. Previously published as *Hazards of Deafness,* and *Silence is Golden, Sometimes.* Roy Holcomb and his sons, Sam and Tom, give an entertaining glimpse of life in the Deaf community that every Deaf reader will relate to and every hearing person will find eye-opening. This humorous compilation offers the reader a communion that no formal discussion of the Deaf experience can ever provide!

DEAF CULTURE, *Our Way* by Roy, Sam and Tom Holcomb
128 pages ◆ 6"x 6"

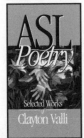

An Important Addition to Every Deaf Studies Collection

Discover ASL poetry through the work of nationally renowned ASL poet Clayton Valli. *ASL Poetry, Selected Works of Clayton Valli* features twenty-one of Valli's poems recited by a variety of signers. Host Lon Kuntze guides the viewer through the hidden meanings in the poems, affording a keen understanding of the material.

ASL Poetry, Selected Works of Clayton Valli *by Clayton Valli*
One 105-minute Video ◆ voice-over

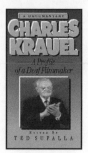

A Flash Back in Deaf Folklore...

ASL linguist Ted Supalla's interest in old films leads you to a rare view of the Deaf community of 70 years ago. As a young man, Charles Krauel bought his first movie camera in 1925 and began recording Deaf community events. He died at the age of 98, leaving behind a rich collection showing the everyday life of Deaf people throughout a half-century. Supalla interviews Krauel and presents selections from his vast film archive in this remarkable video.

Charles Krauel, A Profile of a Deaf Filmmaker *by Ted Supalla*
One 30-minute Video ◆ open-captioned ◆ voice-over

"Good Name Signs Must Suit a Number of Requirements, Many Which Have Never Been Explained in Any Detail"—*Until This Book.*

Learn about the name sign system in the American Deaf Community. *The Book of Name Signs* is a fascinating resource which guides you through the intriguing history and development of the ASL name sign system.

Name signs reveal a part of Deaf culture, and *The Book of Name Signs* is an outstanding, informative, and enjoyable book for learning about them. Included is a list of over 500 appropriately used name signs.

The Book of Name Signs *by Samuel Supalla*
112 pages ◆ 7"x 9"

Hilarious and Touching Clips

Signing Treasures is a special ASL collection from the best-selling *Signing Naturally* educational videos. Choice skits, jokes, stories, legends, poems, and songs are recited by some of the Deaf community's most popular storytellers. *Signing Treasures* brings the ironies, frustrations, and very unique moments of Deaf life into one wonderful videotape.

Signing Treasures *Excerpts from Signing Naturally Videos*
One 50-minute Video ◆ no audio

AND MUCH MORE...

DAWNSIGNPRESS is a publisher of instructional sign language and educational Deaf Studies materials for children and adults, both deaf and hearing. Our list includes exciting books and videotapes on sign language, Deaf culture, as well as children's stories and school materials.

If you would like to know more about DAWNSIGNPRESS products, please write or phone us with the following information:

Name: _____

Address: _____

City/State/Zip: _____

We are also interested in knowing how you liked this guide. Your comments are much appreciated.

_____

_____

_____

_____

DAWNSIGNPRESS

6130 Nancy Ridge Drive, San Diego, California 92121-3223

(619) 626-0600 V/TTY   (619) 625-2336 FAX

ORDER TOLL FREE 1-800-549-5350 V/TTY

PARLI NOTES

PARLI NOTES

PARLI NOTES

PARLI NOTES

PARLI NOTES

PARLI NOTES